Gilbert & Sullivan for Singers

Baritone/Bass

Edited by Richard Walters

T0033979

To access companion recorded accompaniments online, visit:
www.halleonard.com/mylibrary

1222-3582-3835-8588

Cover illustration: W.S. Gilbert created line drawings to accompany his librettos. His childhood nickname was Bab (derived from "baby"), and this was the name he signed to the drawings. They have become known as the "Bab Illustrations." The drawing shown is from *The Pirates of Penzance*: "I am the very model of a modern Major-General."

ISBN 978-0-634-06016-8

HAL•LEONARD®
CORPORATION
7777 W. BLUEMOUND RD. P.O. BOX 13819 MILWAUKEE, WI 53213

Copyright © 2003 by HAL LEONARD CORPORATION
International Copyright Secured   All Rights Reserved

No part of this publication may be reproduced in any form or by any means without the prior
written permission of the publisher.

Visit Hal Leonard Online at
www.halleonard.com

W.S. Gilbert   Arthur Sullivan

Contents

Though this role is usually sung by a baritone, it is possible (because of optional notes) for it to be sung by a tenor; this song appears in both the Tenor and Baritone/Bass volumes of the series.

The price of this publication includes access to companion recorded accompaniments online, for download or streaming, using the unique code found on the title page. Visit **www.halleonard.com/mylibrary** and enter the access code.

Plot Notes

THE GONDOLIERS

or *The King of Barataria*
First produced at the Savoy Theatre, London, on December 7, 1889, with an initial run of 554 performances.

Twenty-four Venetian flower girls are arranging the bouquets they will present to Marco and Giuseppe, the handsomest of all the gondoliers, in hopes of snagging a marriage proposal. The gondoliers decide to choose their brides via a game of blindman's-buff. Happily they end up with the girls they most wanted—Marco with Gianetta and Giuseppe with Tessa. A gondola arrives carrying the Plaza-Toro family. The penniless Duke of Plaza-Toro tells his daughter, Casilda, that as a baby she was married by proxy to the infant son of the King of Barataria. (Casilda loves the drummer Luiz.) The King's Grand Inquisitor, Don Alhambra, explains in **"No Possible Doubt Whatever,"** that he objected to the monarch's religious practices, so he kidnapped the infant prince and took him to Venice to be raised by a gondolier. The prince, who does not know he is a prince, is now himself working as a gondolier in Venice. The court of Barataria has all been killed, and this gondolier is now king, if he can be found. The two newlywed couples return. The Grand Inquisitor is certain that one of the men, Marco or Giuseppe, is the King he seeks, although he can't say which, and takes them both back to Barataria. They will rule jointly until the King's old nursemaid, who is the mother of Luiz, can determine which is the real King.

Act II opens in the Court of Barataria, where the democratic leanings of the joint Kings are immediately apparent. The Kings toil all day for their kingdom and they miss their brides. The brides appear, unable to bear the separation any longer. When the Grand Inquisitor arrives, he explains that this sort of thing had been tried once before to no good end. The Duke arrives with Casilda, who is technically married to one of the two Kings, and Luiz. The three brides ponder the predicament of their two husbands and Casilda's mother tells of her own marriage. The Grand Inquisitor brings in Inez, the nursemaid, to identify the real King. She confesses that when the King was kidnapped she tricked the Grand Inquisitor by substituting her own son. One of the "Kings" is the son of the gondolier Palmieri, the other is the son of the nurse-maid Inez, and the rightful King is Luiz! So the two Kings are gondoliers once again, each happily married to his love. Luiz, now the rightful King, and Casilda happily must be married.

HMS PINAFORE

or *The Lass that Loved a Sailor*
First produced at the Opéra Comique, London, on May 25, 1878, with an initial run of 571 performances.

On the *Pinafore*, anchored off Portsmouth, the crew is proudly polishing and scrubbing the vessel as this satire on British class distinctions and military life opens. A woman named Little Buttercup comes aboard to sell them ribbons and lace for their sweethearts. Despite her merry demeanor, she carries a mysterious secret. Sailor Ralph Rackstraw, the smartest man in the fleet, declares his love for a young maiden. That maiden, unfortunately, is the Captain's daughter. The sailor Dick Deadeye appears with the unkindly explanation that Captains' daughters do not marry mere sailors. Enter the Captain. He explains to Little Buttercup that he is worried because his daughter, Josephine, has refused to marry Sir Joseph Porter, First Lord of the Admiralty. Josephine herself enters, declaring her love for a sailor aboard Pinafore. After her father explains the class issues involved with her romance she promises to forsake the sailor and reconsider Sir Joseph. Sir Joseph enters and introduces himself, offering details of his employment history in **"When I Was a Lad I Served a Term."** Ralph finally summons the courage to confess his love to Josephine, only to have her respond coldly. A heartbroken Ralph threatens to shoot himself, but Josephine relents and confesses that she indeed loves him.

As Act II begins, the Captain paces the deck by night, singing **"Fair Moon, to Thee I Sing."** He confesses his love for Little Buttercup but quickly explains that their different social positions make a relationship impossible. Little Buttercup cryptically advises him not to be too sure of that. Sir Joseph and Josephine enter. Sir Joseph is convinced that Josephine is intimidated by his high social standing; all the while she plots her elopement with Ralph. The evil Dick Deadeye informs the Captain of Josephine's upcoming elopement, allowing the Captain to stop the marriage. The crew steps in on Ralph's behalf, but the Captain curses at this behavior, which brings Sir Joseph out of the woodwork to berate him for speaking so rudely to a British sailor. Once Sir Joseph realizes his love intended to elope with Ralph, he orders the young sailor confined below decks. At the last moment Little Buttercup brings out the truth of her mysterious secret. Apparently she once worked as a nanny of sorts, and made a terrible mistake through which two babies were mixed up. Those babies were the Captain and Ralph. So, in fact, the Captain is a mere sailor and Ralph is the Captain. Her news rings in a happy ending, as Ralph and Josephine as well as the Captain and Little Buttercup are freed from social restrictions and may marry.

IOLANTHE

or *The Peer and the Peri*
First produced at the Savoy Theatre, London, on November 25, 1882, with an initial run of 398 performances.

The lovely fairy women of Arcadia are unhappy in this satire on the House of Lords, because the Fairy Queen has banished Iolanthe for marrying a human. The Queen, who is secretly in love with a human named Private Willis, eventually relents and pardons Iolanthe. Iolanthe returns, looking like a young woman of 17 even though she has a 25-year-old son. Her son, Strephon, is planning to marry Phyllis, the young ward of the Lord Chancellor. But the couple has not received his blessing. The Lord Chancellor and a chorus of nobles march about demanding respect and fanfare. The Lord Chancellor loves Phyllis himself, but fearing the marriage would not be proper he asks the nobles if one of them might marry her. Phyllis announces her objection, adding that her heart has already been given to another. Strephon enters at that moment and announces that he is the object of her affection but the Chancellor dashes his hopes. When Strephon tells his mother of these goings-on, she takes him in her arms to comfort him. Phyllis sees Strephon in the arms of this apparent 17-year-old. Certain she has been betrayed, she becomes engaged to two noblemen. As the act comes to an end, the Fairy Queen decides to send Strephon to Parliament to make nobles out of commoners and generally make life miserable for the Lord Chancellor and the other nobles.

Act II opens on the Westminster Palace Yard and Private Willis singing a merry account of sentinel duty, with **"When All Night Long a Chap Remains."** Strephon has caused an uproar in Parliament, whimsically passing pointless laws. The peers appeal to the fairies. They offer no help but find the peers quite attractive. Despite her love for Willis, the Fairy Queen scolds them for even thinking about marrying mortals. Phyllis meanwhile finds her two fiancées equally uninteresting so she tells them she will choose the one who will forsake his title and give his wealth to the Irish tenantry, which neither will do. Lord Chancellor is suffering from nightmares about love, singing **"When You're Lying Awake with a Dismal Headache."** Strephon eventually convinces Phyllis that Iolanthe is really his mother and they plan to marry immediately. The Lord Chancellor has in the meantime convinced himself that it be acceptable for him to marry his ward. But Iolanthe steps forward to confess that she is his long-lost wife. The Queen is about to order Iolanthe's execution for this marriage, when the fairies step forward to announce they have all married nobles. To save them all from execution, the Lord Chancellor rewrites the law so that any fairy who does not marry a mortal will be condemned to death. The Queen happily marries Private Willis to save her own life. Wings sprout from the nobles' shoulders as the House of Peers becomes the House of Peri.

6

THE MIKADO

or The Town of Titipu
First produced at the Savoy Theatre, London, on March 14, 1885, with an initial run of 672 performances.

The setting for this most popular of Savoy operettas is the courtyard of the Japanese Lord High Executioner in the town of Titipu. Handsome Nanki-Poo, a wandering minstrel, runs in looking for the lovely Yum-Yum. He has loved Yum-Yum for a long time and now that Ko-Ko, Yum-Yum's guardian and fiancée, is to be beheaded he sees his opportunity. However, Ko-Ko has been reprieved, and enters to announce his new appointment as Lord High Executioner, singing **"As Some Day It May Happen."** As he discusses his wedding plans, Yum-Yum and two school-mates enter. Nanki-Poo apologizes to Ko-Ko for being in love Yum-Yum, receiving forgiveness. Later, Yum-Yum confesses to Nanki-Poo that she does not love Ko-Ko. Nanki-Poo confesses that he is actually son of the Mikado and is traveling in disguise to avoid marrying an elderly woman who mistook his good nature for affectionate advances. The Mikado meanwhile has sent word to Ko-Ko that if he doesn't execute someone soon his title will be abolished and the town reduced to a mere village. Ko-Ko spots Nanki-Poo about to end his life over his hopeless love, and asks if he might execute him since the lad is about do himself in anyway. Nanki-Poo agrees on the condition that he be allowed to marry Yum-Yum and live with her for one month before the execution. Ko-Ko agrees, being a more practical than romantic man. When Katisha, the elderly woman who wants to marry Nanki-Poo, arrives and tries to tell everyone of his true identity, she is ignored.

Act II opens on the preparations for Yum-Yum's wedding. Obsessed with her own beauty, she wonders why she should be so much more attractive than anyone else. But happiness dims when Ko-Ko learns that by law she, as the widow of Nanki-Poo, must be buried alive following his execution. A bribe to the Pooh-Bah (also known as the Lord High Everything Else) to fake a certificate of execution seems the best course of action until the Mikado arrives. When Katisha sees the execution certificate and tells the Mikado that his son has been executed, the Mikado promises punishment to all involved. Ko-Ko goes to Nanki-Poo for advice. Nanki-Poo advises him to marry Katisha. Ko-Ko bizarrely woos Katisha, singing **"Willow, Tit-Willow,"** and soon the two join in duet and then in marriage. Nanki-Poo, now free from Katisha's clutches, comes out of hiding and introduces the Mikado to his new daughter-in-law and thus ends the threat of punishment and the operetta.

THE PIRATES OF PENZANCE

or The Slave of Duty
One performance, for copyright purposes, was given on December 30, 1879, at the Royal Bijou Theatre in Paighton, Devonshire. It opened officially for a run in New York at the Fifth Avenue Theatre on December 31, 1879. The London premiere was at the Opéra Comique on April 3, 1880, with an initial run of 363 performances.

Pirate festivities on the Cornwall coast open this satire on British military and constabulary, celebrating the completion of young Frederic's pirate internship. But Frederic is dejected. His situation is explained by Ruth, who had been his nursemaid. It seems that Ruth, being quite hard of hearing, mistook Frederic's father's instruction to apprentice him as a pilot and instead set him up as a pirate. The heartbroken Frederic must, for duty's sake, return to the honest world and work to end piracy even though this means betraying his pirate friends. He begs the pirates to give up their life of crime but they decline, as the Pirate King sings of the joys of pirating in **"I Am a Pirate King."** Ruth begs Frederic to take her with him, as he has never seen another woman and considers the aging Ruth to be beautiful. Just then a party of beautiful young maidens appear for a picnic and are shocked to find a pirate in their midst. He pleads with them to take pity on him. Just when it appears that all will reject him, Mabel appears and bravely offers him her heart. The other pirates spot the lovely maidens and creep in to kidnap them. The girls' father appears, announcing **"I Am the Very Model of a Modern Major-General,"** thereby hoping to foil the pirates' plans of marriage. When that fails he plays on his knowledge that Pirates of Penzance are orphans and are always tenderhearted toward other orphans. He explains that he too is an orphan and would be lost and lonely without his daughters. The pirates relent and the Major-General, Frederic and the girls depart, leaving poor Ruth with the pirates.

Act II opens in a ruined chapel, where the Major-General confesses to Frederic and Mabel that he is not actually an orphan. Frederic explains his plans to put the pirates out of business, and is in the process of proposing to Mabel when policemen arrive on their way to conquer the pirates themselves. They are just describing their grand plans when Ruth and the Pirate King arrive with a most ingenious paradox.

Apparently Frederic was born on a leap-year day, so he won't actually reach his 21st birthday until 1940. Therefore he is still the pirates' apprentice. Always a slave to duty, Frederic returns to his pirate life, where honor forces him to tell the pirates that the Major-General is not an orphan. The policemen reappear and reluctantly prepare to arrest the pirates, as the Sergeant sings **"The Policeman's Song."** The pirates meanwhile can be heard sneaking up on the Major-General. Just as the pirates are about to do in the Major-General, the policemen leap to his defense, only to be defeated almost immediately. They are about to be killed when the police pull Union Jacks from their pockets and command the pirates to stand down in the name of Queen Victoria. The pirates, who love their Queen, comply. Ruth puts everything to rights by explaining that the pirates are actually noblemen who have gone wrong. They are immediately forgiven and given back their titles. Frederic and Mabel reunite and the Major-General asks the pirates/nobles to marry his daughters.

PRINCESS IDA

or *Castle Adamant*

First produced at the Savoy Theatre, London, on January 5, 1884, with an initial run of 246 performances. *Princess Ida* is the only three-act operetta by Gilbert and Sullivan.

This satire on women's suffrage and Darwin's evolutionary theories opens on a scene of great expectation. Prince Hilarion awaits the arrival of Princess Ida, to whom he has been betrothed since infancy. But her father, King Gama, arrives without her. He sings **"If You Give Me Your Attention,"** explaining to the Prince and his father King Hildebrand that Princess Ida is now running a school for girls at Castle Adamant. There they study the classics and the villainy of men. Hildebrand and Hilarion decide to hold Gama and his three sons as hostages while they storm the Castle Adamant to claim the Princess.

Hilarion and two friends scale the castle wall and disguise themselves in women's clothing. With several of the women aware of the men, and keeping their secret, the three pull off the ruse for a time. But after drinking a bit too much, one of the men gives up the secret. Princess Ida orders the men's arrest. But King Hildebrand has massed his troops outside the castle walls to force Ida to make good on the betrothal. He gives her twenty-four hours to make up her mind, threatening to raze the castle and hang her brothers and father if she declines.

The Princess decides to fight, but her students are in terror of hurting someone so they refuse. King Gama returns, crestfallen after such obsequious treatment at the Hildebrand palace, singing **"Whene're I Spoke."** Meanwhile King Hildebrand has decided that fighting women is in poor form, so he has Ida's brothers brought from his castle to fight for the women against Prince Hilarion and his two friends. Hilarion and company win. Princess Ida marries Hilarion, and two of her colleagues marry his friends. Lady Blanche is left to fulfill her dream of running the school and the curtain falls.

RUDDIGORE

or *The Witch's Curse*

First produced at the Savoy Theatre, London, on March 14, 1885, with an initial run of 288 performances.

The professional bridesmaids in the Cornish village of Rederring are antsy for work. The lovely Rose Maybud is the most likely candidate, but she keeps rejecting suitors. She explains that she is waiting for the right person. Rose's Aunt Hannah tells of Sir Roderic Murgatroyd of Ruddigore, her lost love. Roderic defied the curse of the Murgatroyd heirs, which condemns them to commit a crime each day or perish, and died on their wedding day. Despard Murgatroyd has assumed the title and is living the obligatory life of crime. The shy Robin Oakapple, who is really Sir Ruthven Murgatroyd, appears. Robin explains that he is too shy to approach Rose, singing **"My Boy, You May Take It from Me."** Robin's half brother, a sailor named Richard, offers to woo Rose on Robin's behalf, but falls madly in love with her and woos her for himself instead. When Robin learns of this betrayal he poisons Rose's mind against sailors and she turns her affections to him. At this point Mad Margaret enters. Driven to insanity by her passion for Despard, she is wildly jealous of Rose, who reassures her. The plot thickens when Robin reveals himself as Despard's older brother, whom all thought was dead. Robin's title is restored and Rose leaves him for Despard. But Despard spurns her, going back to Margaret. Rose returns to Richard and Robin collapses.

Act II opens with a haggard Sir Ruthven (Robin) in the picture gallery of his castle, looking for a crime to commit. Rose and Richard have come to ask permission to marry and Ruthven threatens to imprison Rose as his crime of the day. Richard pulls out a Union Jack, which of course even the worst of criminals cannot ignore, and the two leave safely. At this point, the portraits of the previously cursed Murgatroyds come to life to remind Ruthven what will happen if he fails to commit a crime. Ruthven wearily sends someone off to kidnap a maiden on his behalf, which brings Hannah to the castle. In the meantime Despard and Margaret, now school masters, arrive to encourage Ruthven to reform. They add that under the law Ruthven is responsible for Despard's crime as well as his own. Ruthven vows to reform, no matter what the consequences. With Hannah in the room, Ruthven calls upon the picture of his Uncle Roderic to help him. Roderic's picture comes to life and he spots Hannah. Ruthven leaves, contemplating his predicament. But the day is saved when Ruthven rushes back in with a brainstorm. Failing to commit a crime each day while knowing the sentence for such action is death, he reasons, is tantamount to suicide. Since suicide is a crime in and of itself, Sir Roderic should never have died. This means that all concerned may pair off as they see fit and thus ends the curse and the operetta.

THE SORCERER

First produced at the Opéra Comique, London, on November 17, 1877, with an initial run of 178 performances.

The village of Ploverleigh is percolating with affection as this satire on Victorian society opens. Villager Constance Partlet harbors secret feelings for Dr. Daly, the Vicar. Daly sings **"Time Was, When Love and I,"** oblivious of Constance's feelings. Constance's mother, meanwhile, has her eye on the Notary. Aline Sangazure glories in her engagement to Alexis Poindextre of the Grenadier Guards. Aline and Alexis, hoping to share their loving bliss with the entire village, hire a sorcerer to drug the community with a love-at-first-sight potion. The sorcerer introduces himself with **"My Name Is John Wellington Wells."** The potion is administered through tea at a village picnic. Everyone but the young lovers and the sorcerer drinks the potion-spiked tea and falls into a deep sleep.

As midnight strikes the villagers begin to awaken, immediately falling head-over-heels in love with the first person they happen to spot. Seeing the potion's effects, Alexis asks Aline to drink the potion, to deepen their love for each other. She refuses, causing a quarrel. Eventually she agrees, but spots Dr. Daly immediately afterward and falls in love with him instead of her betrothed Alexis. Dr. Daly, confused, sings **"Engaged to So-and-So,"** accompanying himself on a flageolet. The potion-induced romances have made a mess of things. Alexis' father, Sir Marmaduke has fallen for Mrs. Partlet, while Lady Sangazure has become smitten with Mr. Wells and Constance with the Notary. It becomes apparent that either Alexis or Mr. Wells must give his life to the forces of evil to break the spell. Neither is willing so a vote is taken. The sorcerer loses and is swallowed up by the earth as a gong sounds. The potion's spell is broken and the villagers return to their original affections.

THE YEOMEN OF THE GUARD
or *The Merryman and His Maid*
First produced at the Savoy Theatre, London, on October 3, 1888, with an initial run of 423 performances.

The year is fifteen-hundred-and-something. Young Phoebe Meryll ponders the heartbreaks of love. She is pining for the dashing Colonel Fairfax who sits in the Tower of London awaiting execution for the crime of sorcery. He was accused of the crime by his scheming cousin. Should he die without a wife, Fairfax explains to the Lieutenant, his title and wealth transfer to the cousin. He begs the Lieutenant to marry him to the poorest woman that can be found so that she might inherit his name and wealth instead. Meanwhile Wilfred, Head Jailor and Assistant Tormentor of the Tower of London, has eyes for Phoebe. While she once thought him fine, she has since become enamored of the Colonel and will have nothing to with Wilfred. Jester Jack Point and singer Elsie Maynard enter. A less than appreciative crowd threatens to mob them but the Lieutenant saves them, immediately marrying Elsie to Fairfax. Jack describes his profession with **"I've Jibe and Joke."** Meanwhile, Phoebe has come up with a plan. She flirts with Wilfrid and steals his keys just long enough for her father to free Fairfax. Wilfrid is barely gone when Fairfax appears in the uniform of the Yeomen of the Guard, posing as the son of Sergeant Meryll. As Phoebe and her "brother" give each other an uncommonly affectionate greeting, the bells toll the hour of the execution. Guards rush back with the news that Fairfax has escaped.

Act II finds Jack Point feeling regret for allowing Elsie to marry Fairfax. It seemed a better idea when Fairfax was about to die, since Jack wanted to marry Elsie himself and figured Fairfax's money would be welcome. He advises Wilfrid on the hazards of jesting. The newly freed Fairfax is putting the fidelity of his new wife to the test, masquerading as Leonard Meryll. Jack and Wilfrid conspire to fake Fairfax's death, saying that they shot the Colonel as he dove into the river. With Fairfax thought dead, Jack proposes to Elsie, who rejects him. Fairfax wonders who his new bride might be, only to discover moments later that his bride is Elsie. Phoebe, distraught over loosing Fairfax tells Wilfrid of the escape and disguise. Wilfrid forces her to marry him to keep the secret. Suddenly the real Leonard appears with an official pardon for Fairfax. Elsie, at first heartbroken to learn that her real husband is alive is delighted when it is revealed that her beloved Leonard is really Fairfax and therefore they are married. Jack, the only one left without a spouse, falls to the ground in a faint.

No Possible Doubt Whatever

THE GONDOLIERS

Words by W.S. Gilbert
Music by Arthur Sullivan

Copyright © 2001 by HAL LEONARD CORPORATION
International Copyright Secured   All Rights Reserved

12

Both of the babes were strong ___ and stout, And con - sid - er - ring all things,
Which was which he could nev - er make out, De - spite his best en -
taste for drink, com - bined ___ with gout Had dou - bled him up for
in and out and round ___ a - bout And you'll dis - cov - er

clev - er. Of *that* there is no man - ner of doubt No
deav - our. Of *that* there is no man - ner of doubt No
ev - er. Of *that* there is no man - ner of doubt No
nev - er. A tale so free from ev - er - y doubt All

prob - a - ble, pos - si - ble shad - ow of doubt No pos - si - ble doubt what -
prob - a - ble, pos - si - ble shad - ow of doubt No pos - si - ble doubt what -
prob - a - ble, pos - si - ble shad - ow of doubt No pos - si - ble doubt what -
prob - a - ble, pos - si - ble shad - ow of doubt All pos - si - ble doubt what -

ev – er!   No pos – si – ble doubt what – ev – er!
ev – er!   No pos – si – ble doubt what – ev – er!
ev – er!   No pos – si – ble doubt what – ev – er!

2. But   ev – er!   A tale so free from
3. Time
4. The

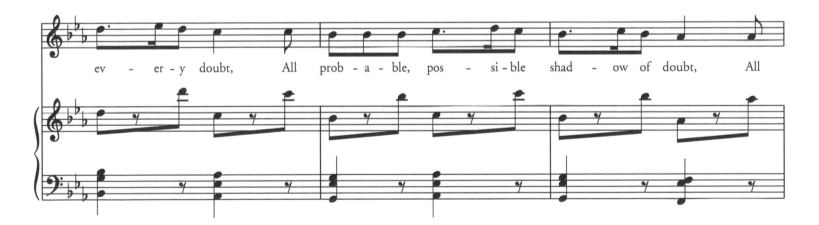

ev – er – y doubt,   All prob – a – ble, pos – si – ble shad – ow of doubt,   All

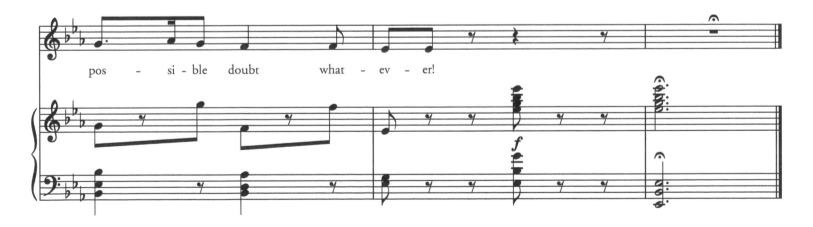

pos – si – ble doubt what – ev – er!

When All Night Long a Chap Remains

IOLANTHE

Words by W.S. Gilbert
Music by Arthur Sullivan

Copyright © 2001 by HAL LEONARD CORPORATION
International Copyright Secured   All Rights Reserved

is,   as - sum - ing that he's   got   an - y.   Tho' nev - er nur -   tured
vote   just   as   their lead - ers   tell 'em to.   But   then the   pros -   pect

in   the lap Of   lux - u - ry,   yet I ad - mon - ish you,   I
of   a   lot Of   dull M. P.'s   in close prox - im - i - ty,   All

am an in - tel - lec - tual chap, And think of things that would as -
think - ing for them - selves, is what No man can face with e - qua -

Tempo primo ♩ = 69

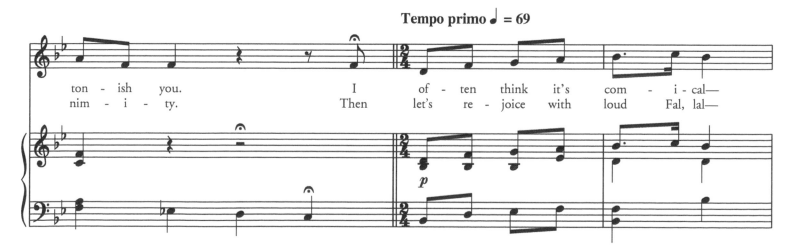

ton - ish you.   I   of - ten think it's com - i - cal—
nim - i - ty.   Then let's re - joice with loud Fal, lal—

p

Fal, lal, ___ la! Fal, lal, ___ la! How
Fal, lal, ___ la! Fal, lal, ___ la! That { Na - ture al - ways

does con - trive— Fal, lal, ___ la, la! That ___

ev - 'ry boy and ___ ev - 'ry gal That's born in - to the ___

poco rit.

world a - live Is ei - ther a lit - tle Lib - er - al Or

poco rit.

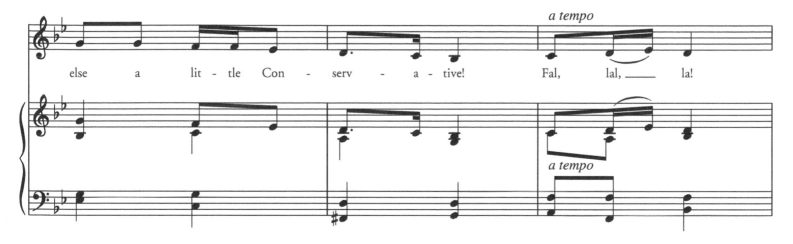

else a lit - tle Con - serv - a - tive! Fal, lal, ___ la!

Fal, lal, ___ la! Is ei - ther a lit - tle Lib - er - al Or

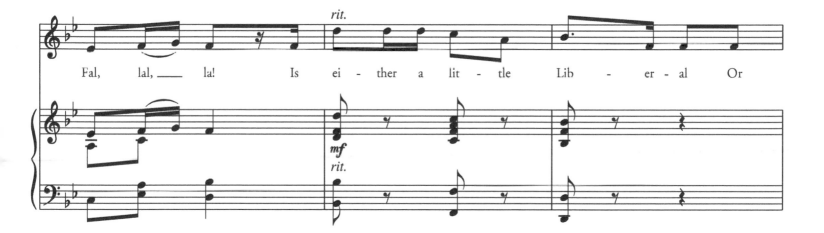

else a lit - tle Con - serv - a - tive! Fal, lal, la!

2. When

17

When You're Lying Awake with a Dismal Headache

IOLANTHE

Words by W.S. Gilbert
Music by Arthur Sullivan

Allegro ♩. = 126

Recit.
LORD CHANCELLOR *(very miserable):*

a tempo

Love, un-re-quit-ed, robs me of my rest:

Love, hope-less love, my ar-dent soul en-cum-bers:

Copyright © 2001 by HAL LEONARD CORPORATION
International Copyright Secured   All Rights Reserved

Love, night-mare-like, lies heav-y on my chest, And

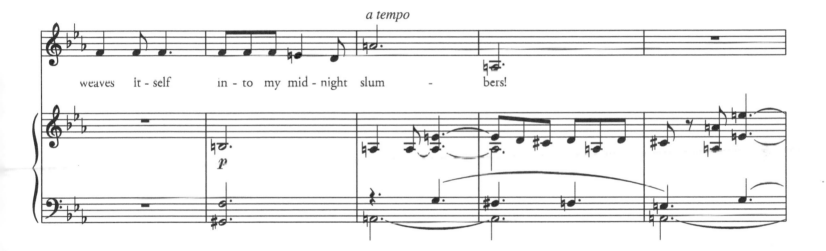

a tempo

weaves it-self in-to my mid-night slum - bers!

Allegro ma non troppo ♩. = 100

When you're

ly - ing a - wake with a dis - mal head - ache, and re - pose is ta - boo'd by anx - i - e - ty, I con -

ceive you may use an - y lan - guage you choose to in - dulge in, with - out im - pro - pri - e - ty; For your

brain is on fire ___ the bed - clothes con - spire ___ of u - su - al slum - ber to plun - der you: First your

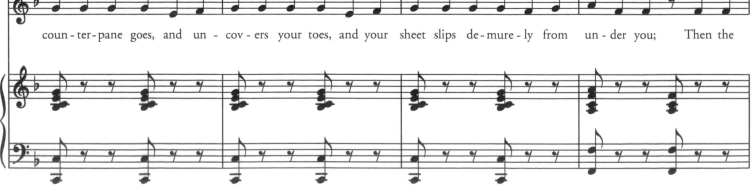

coun - ter - pane goes, and un - cov - ers your toes, and your sheet slips de - mure - ly from un - der you; Then the

21

get some re-pose in the form of a doze, with hot eye-balls and head ev - er ach-ing, But your

slum-ber-ing teems with such hor - ri - ble dreams that you'd ver - y much bet - ter be wak-ing; For you

dream you are cross-ing the Chan-nel, and toss-ing a - bout in a steam-er from Har-wich— Which is

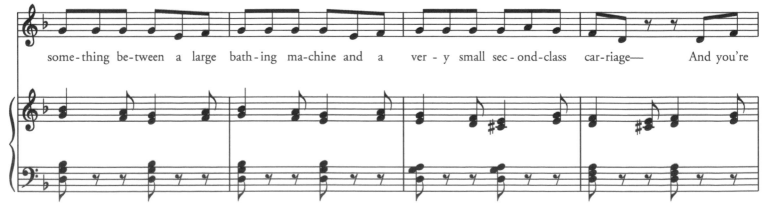

some-thing be-tween a large bath-ing ma-chine and a ver - y small sec-ond-class car-riage— And you're

driv-ing like mad with this sin-gu-lar lad (by-the-bye, the ship's now a four-wheel-er), And you're

play-ing round games, and he calls you bad names when you tell him that "ties pay the deal-er"; But

this you can't stand, so you throw up your hand, and you find you're as cold as an i-ci-cle; In your

shirt and your socks (the black silk with gold clocks), cross-ing Sal's-bu-ry Plain on a bi-cy-cle: And

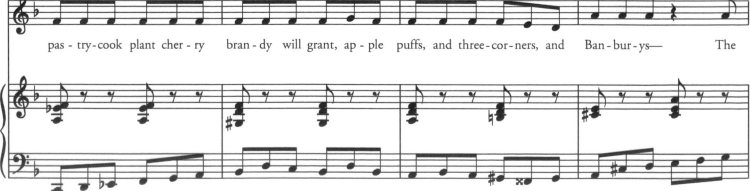

cramp in your toes, and a fly on your nose, and some fluff in your lung, and a fe - ver - ish tongue, and a

dim.

thirst that's in - tense, and a gen - er - al sense that you have - n't been sleep - ing in clo - ver;

cresc.

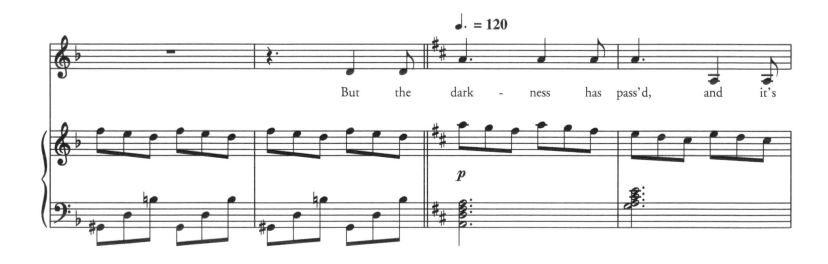

♩. = 120

But the dark - ness has pass'd, and it's

p

day - light at last, and the night has been long— dit - to,

cresc.

a piacere

dit - to my song— And thank good - ness they're

f colla voce

(*Lord Chancellor falls exhausted on a seat.*)

both of them o - ver!

Con fuoco

ff

Fair Moon, to Thee I Sing

HMS PINAFORE

Words by W.S. Gilbert
Music by Arthur Sullivan

Moderato

CAPTAIN CORCORAN:

Fair moon, to thee I sing, Bright re-gent of the

heav-ens, Say, why is ev-'ry-thing

Copyright © 2001 by HAL LEONARD CORPORATION
International Copyright Secured   All Rights Reserved

Ei - ther at six - es or at sev - ens? Say, why is

ev - 'ry - thing _____ Ei - ther at six - es or at sev - ens? I have

lived hith - er - to Free from the breath _ of ___

slan - der, Be - loved by all my crew, A

real - ly pop-u-lar com-mand - er. But now my kind-ly crew re-

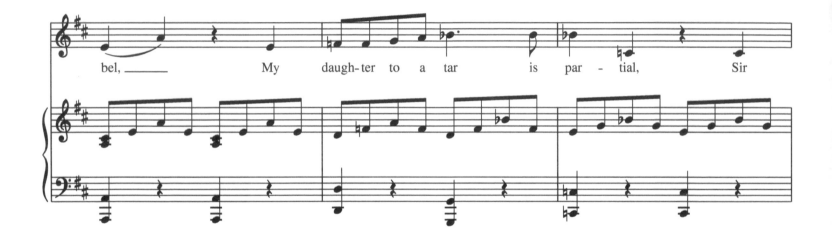

bel, _____ My daugh-ter to a tar is par - tial, Sir

Jo - seph storms, and, sad to tell, He threat-ens ____ a court-

cresc.

mar - tial! Fair moon, to thee __ I __ sing,

f *p*

f dim. *pp*

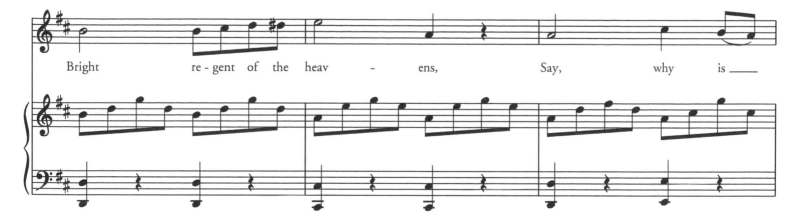

Bright re-gent of the heav - ens, Say, why is

ev - 'ry - thing Ei - ther at six - es or at sev - ens?

rall.
opt.
Fair moon, to thee I sing, Bright re - gent of the
colla voce

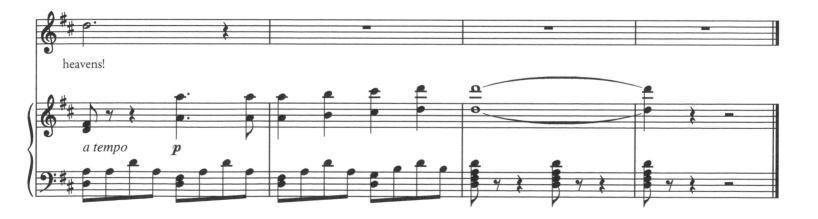

heavens!
a tempo *p*

When I Was a Lad I Served a Term

HMS PINAFORE

Words by W.S. Gilbert
Music by Arthur Sullivan

Allegro non troppo

SIR JOSEPH:

1. When
2. As
3. In
4. Of

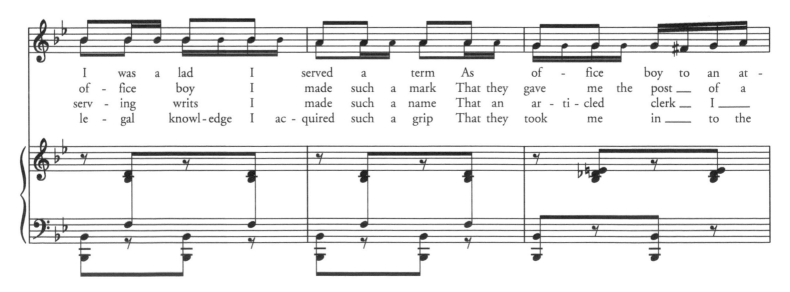

I	was	a	lad	I	served	a	term	As	of-	fice	boy	to	an	at-
of-	fice	boy	I	made	such	a	mark	That they	gave	me	the	post	of	a
serv-	ing	writs	I	made	such	a	name	That an	ar-	ti-	cled	clerk	I
le-	gal	knowl-edge	I	ac-	quired	such	a	grip	That they	took	me	in	to the

Copyright © 2001 by HAL LEONARD CORPORATION
International Copyright Secured   All Rights Reserved

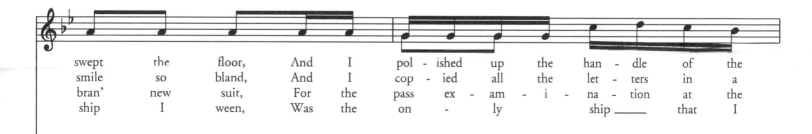

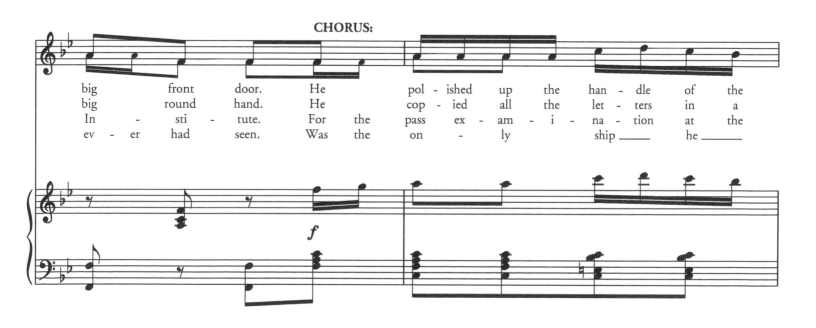

SIR:

big front door. I pol - ished up that han - dle so
big round hand. I cop - ied all the let - ters in a
In - sti - tute. That pass ex - am - i - na - tion did so
ev - er had seen. But that kind of ship so

p

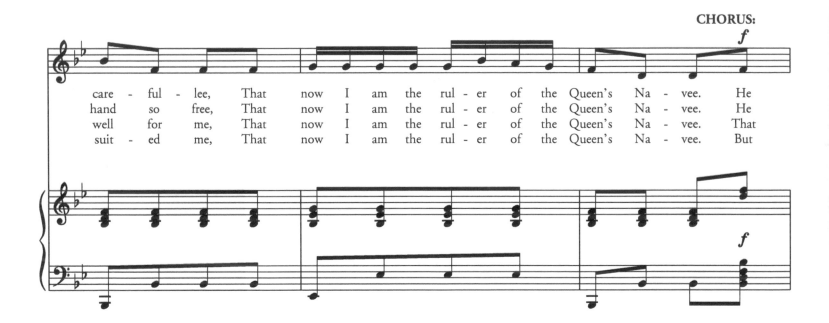

CHORUS: *f*

care - ful - lee, That now I am the rul - er of the Queen's Na - vee. He
hand so free, That now I am the rul - er of the Queen's Na - vee. He
well for me, That now I am the rul - er of the Queen's Na - vee. That
suit - ed me, That now I am the rul - er of the Queen's Na - vee. But

f

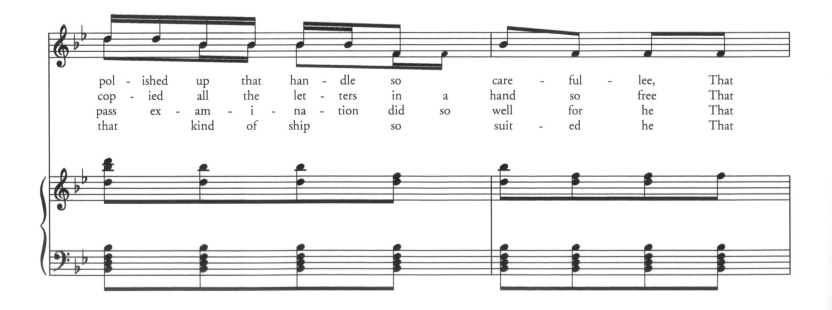

pol - ished up that han - dle so care - ful - lee, That
cop - ied all the let - ters in a hand so free That
pass ex - am - i - na - tion did so well for he That
that kind of ship so suit - ed he That

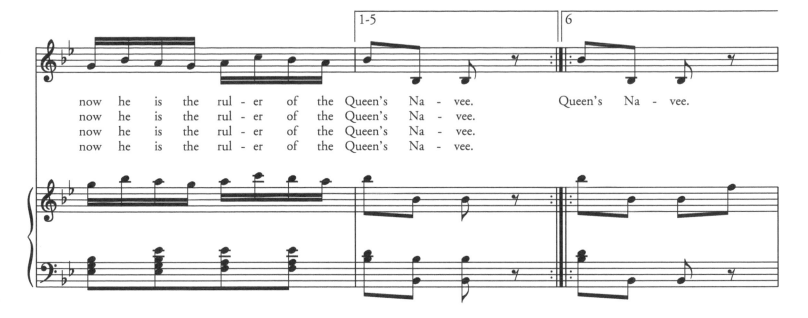

now he is the rul - er of the Queen's Na - vee.   Queen's Na - vee.
now he is the rul - er of the Queen's Na - vee.
now he is the rul - er of the Queen's Na - vee.
now he is the rul - er of the Queen's Na - vee.

5. I grew so rich that I was sent
   By a pocket borough into Parliament.
   I always voted at my party's call,
   And I never thought of thinking for myself at all.
   I thought so little they rewarded me,
   By making me the ruler of the Queen's Navee.

     CHORUS.— He thought so little, etc.

6. Now landsmen all, whoever you may be,
   If you want to rise to the top of the tree,
   If your soul isn't fettered to an office stool,
   Be careful to be guided by this golden rule,—
   Stick close to your desks and never go to sea,
   And you all may be rulers of the Queen's Navee.

     CHORUS.— Stick close, etc.

Willow, Tit-Willow
THE MIKADO

Words by W.S. Gilbert
Music by Arthur Sullivan

Copyright © 2001 by HAL LEONARD CORPORATION
International Copyright Secured   All Rights Reserved

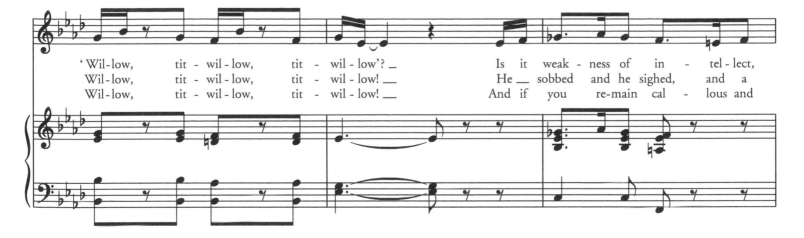

‘Wil-low, tit - wil-low, tit - wil-low’? _ Is it weak-ness of in - tel-lect,
Wil-low, tit - wil-low, tit - wil-low! _ He _ sobbed and he sighed, and a
Wil-low, tit - wil-low, tit - wil-low! _ And if you re-main cal - lous and

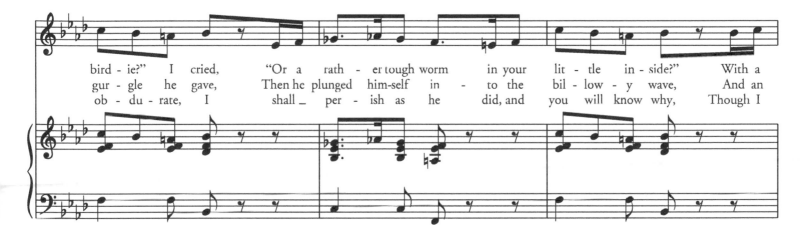

bird - ie?” I cried, “Or a rath - er tough worm in your lit - tle in - side?” With a
gur - gle he gave, Then he plunged him-self in - to the bil - low - y wave, And an
ob - du - rate, I shall _ per - ish as he did, and you will know why, Though I

shake of his poor lit - tle head he re - plied, “Oh, wil - low, tit - wil - low, tit -
ech - o a - rose from the su - i-cide’s grave— “Oh, wil - low, tit - wil - low, tit -
prob - a - bly shall not ex - claim as I die, “Oh, wil - low, tit - wil - low, tit -

1, 2

wil-low!” _
wil-low!” _

3

2. He
3. Now I wil-low!” _

pp

As Some Day It May Happen

THE MIKADO

Words by W.S. Gilbert
Music by Arthur Sullivan

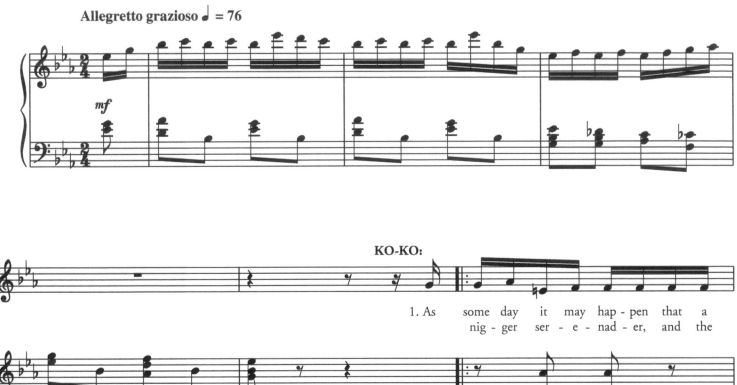

Allegretto grazioso ♩ = 76

KO-KO:

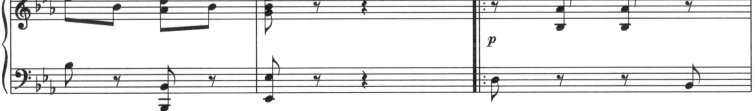

1. As some day it may hap-pen that a
nig - ger ser - e - nad - er, and the

vic - tim must be found, I've got a lit - tle list— I've got a lit - tle list of so -
oth - ers of his race, And the pia - no - or - gan - ist— I've got him on the list! And the

Copyright © 2001 by HAL LEONARD CORPORATION
International Copyright Secured   All Rights Reserved

ci - e - ty of - fend - ers who might well be un - der-ground, And who nev - er would be missed— who
peo - ple who eat pep - per - mint and puff it in your face, They nev - er would be missed— they

nev - er would be missed! There's the pes - ti - len - tial nui - san - ces who write for au - to-graphs— All
nev - er would be missed! Then the id - i - ot who prais - es, with en - thu - si - as - tic tone, All

peo - ple who have flab - by hands and ir - ra - tat - ing laughs— All chil-dren who are up in dates, and
cen - tu - ries but this, and ev - 'ry coun-try but his own; And the la - dy from the prov - in - ces, who

floor you with 'em flat— All per - sons who in shak - ing hands, shake hands with you like *that*— And
dress - es like a guy, And "who does - n't think she danc - es, but would rath - er like to try"; And that

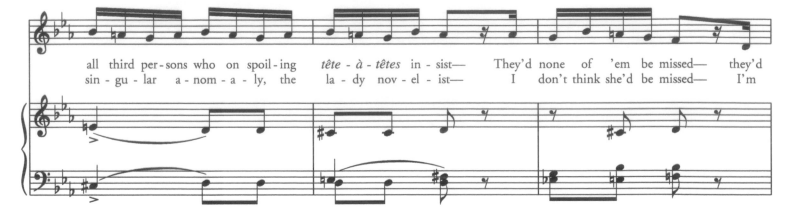

all third per-sons who on spoil-ing *tête - à - têtes* in - sist— They'd none of 'em be missed— they'd
sin - gu - lar a-nom-a-ly, the la - dy nov-el-ist— I don't think she'd be missed— I'm

none of 'em be missed! I've got 'em on the list— I've got 'em on the list; And they'll
sure she'd not be missed! I've got her on the list— I've got her on the list; And I

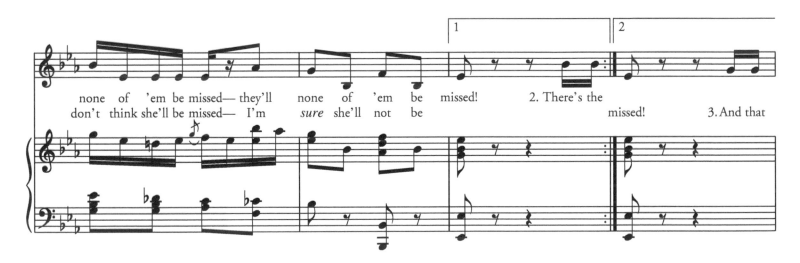

none of 'em be missed— they'll none of 'em be missed! 2. There's the
don't think she'll be missed— I'm *sure* she'll not be missed! 3. And that

Ni - si Pri - us nui-sance, who just now is rath - er rife, The ju - di - cial hu - mor - ist— I've

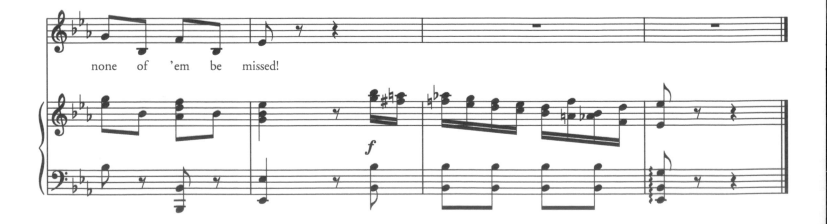

The Policeman's Song

THE PIRATES OF PENZANCE

Words by W.S. Gilbert
Music by Arthur Sullivan

SERGEANT:

1. When a fel-on's not en-gaged in his em-ploy-ment (his em-ploy-ment),* Or ma-turing his fe-lo-nious lit-tle plans, (lit-tle plans), His ca-
2. When the en-ter-pris-ing bur-glar's not a-bur-gling (not a-bur-gling), When the cut-throat is-n't oc-cu-pied in crime, (—pied in crime), He ____

The parenthetical phrases are chorus responses, but may be sung in a solo version of the song.

Copyright © 2001 by HAL LEONARD CORPORATION
International Copyright Secured   All Rights Reserved

one con - sid - er - a - tion with an - oth - er (with an - oth - er)! A po -

lice - man's lot is not a hap - py one; Ah, When con - sta - bu - lar - y du - ty's to be

done, to be done, The po - lice - man's lot is not a hap - py one, hap - py one!

p

I Am a Pirate King

THE PIRATES OF PENZANCE

Words by W.S. Gilbert
Music by Arthur Sullivan

Allegro moderato

PIRATE KING:

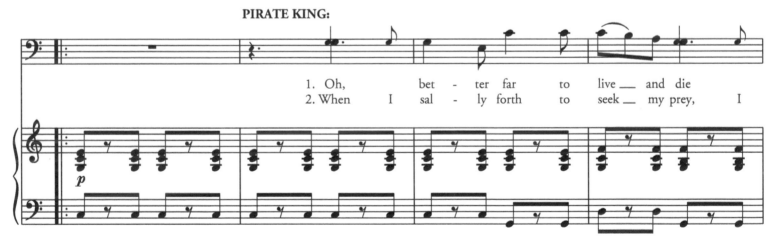

1. Oh, bet - ter far to live __ and die
2. When I sal - ly forth to seek __ my prey, I

Un - der the brave black flag I fly, Than play a sanc - ti -
help my - self in a roy - al way. I sink a few more

Copyright © 2001 by HAL LEONARD CORPORATION
International Copyright Secured   All Rights Reserved

mo - nious part, With a pi - rate head and a pi - rate heart.
ships, __ it's true, Than a well - bred mon - arch ought to do;

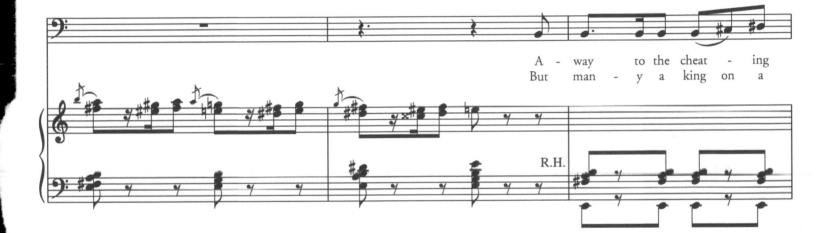

A - way to the cheat - ing
But man - y a king on a

world go you,
first - class throne,

Where
If he

pi - rates all __ are well - to - do; But I'll be true to the
wants to call __ his crown his own, Must man - age some - how

cresc.

50

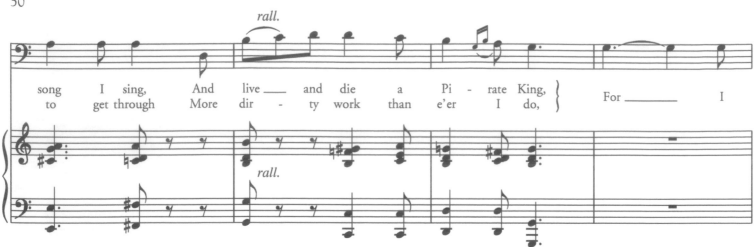

song   I   sing,   And   live ___ and   die   a   Pi - rate   King, }   For ____   I
to   get through   More   dir - ty   work   than   e'er   I   do, }

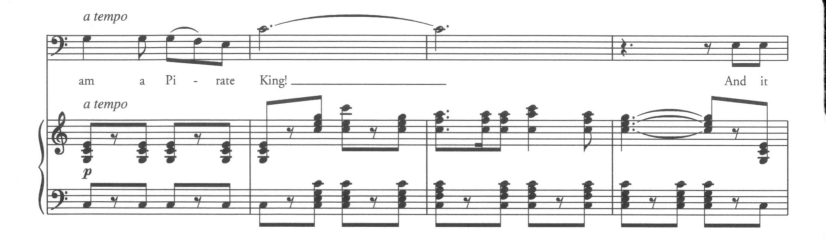

am   a   Pi - rate   King! _____   And   it

is,   it   is   a   glo - rious   thing ___   To   be   a   Pi - rate

King! _____   For   I   am   a   Pi - rate   King! _____

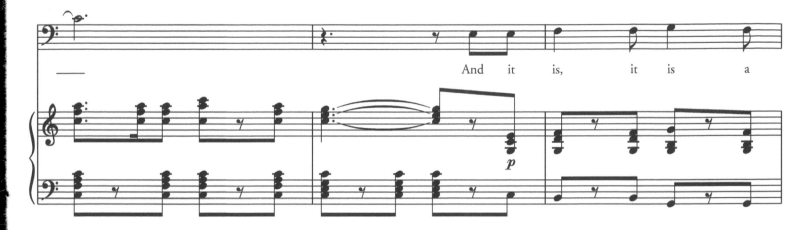

And it is, it is a

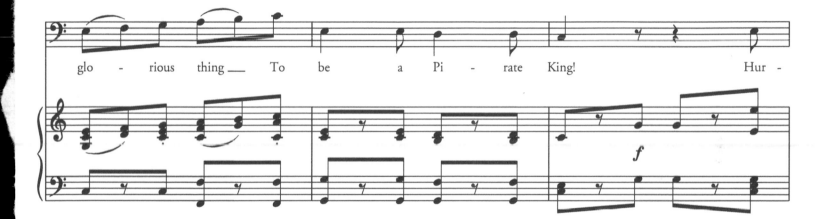

glo - rious thing — To be a Pi - rate King! Hur -

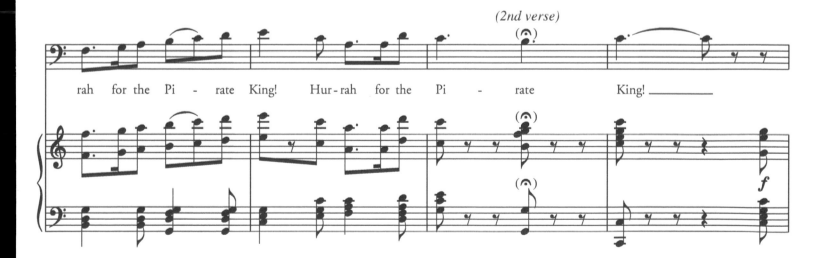

rah for the Pi - rate King! Hur-rah for the Pi - rate King! _____

(2nd verse)

I Am the Very Model
of a Modern Major-General

THE PIRATES OF PENZANCE

Words by W.S. Gilbert
Music by Arthur Sullivan

Copyright © 2001 by HAL LEONARD CORPORATION
International Copyright Secured   All Rights Reserved

am the ver - y mod - el of a mod - ern Ma - jor - Gen - er - al; I've
know our myth - ic his - to - ry, King Ar - thur's and Sir Car - a - doc's; I

in - for - ma - tion veg - e - ta - ble, an - i - mal, and min - er - al; I
an - swer hard a - cros - tics; I've a pret - ty taste for par - a - dox; I

know the kings of Eng - land, and I quote the fights his - tor - i - cal, From
quote, in el - e - gi - acs, all the crimes of He - lio - gab - a - lus; In

Mar - a - thon to Wa - ter - loo, in or - der cat - e - gor - i - cal; I'm
con - ics I can floor pe - cu - li - ar - i - ties pa - rab - o - lous; I can

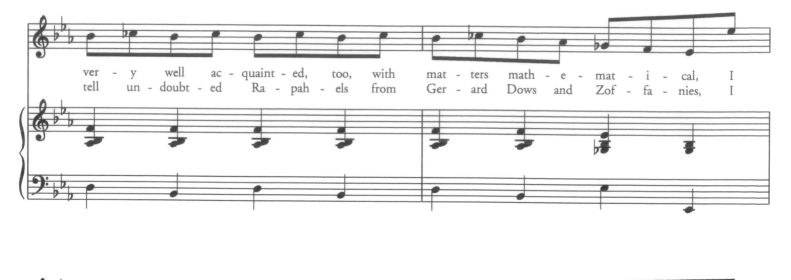

ver - y well ac - quaint - ed, too, with mat - ters math - e - mat - i - cal, I
tell un - doubt - ed Ra - pah - els from Ger - ard Dows and Zof - fa - nies, I

un - der - stand e - qua - tions, both the sim - ple and quad - rat - i - cal, A -
know the croak - ing cho - rus from the *Frogs* of Ar - is - toph - a - nes! Then

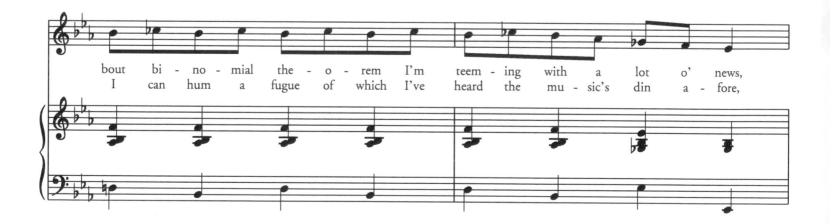

bout bi - no - mial the - o - rem I'm teem - ing with a lot o' news,
I can hum a fugue of which I've heard the mu - sic's din a - fore,

(Bothered for next rhyme— struck with an idea— joyfully)

With man - y cheer - ful facts a - bout the
And whis - tle all the airs from that in -

CHORUS:

square of the hy - pot - e - nuse. With man - y cheer - ful facts a - bout the
fer - nal non - sense, *Pin - a - fore!* And whis - tle all the airs from that in -

square of the hy - pot - e - nuse, With man - y cheer - ful facts a - bout the
fer - nal non - sense, *Pin - a - fore,* And whis - tle all the airs from that in -

square of the hy - pot - e - nuse, With man - y cheer - ful facts a - bout the
fer - nal non - sense, *Pin - a - fore,* And whis - tle all the airs from that in -

square of the hy - pot - e - pot - e - nuse.
fer - nal non - sense, *Pin - a - pin - a - fore.*

MG:

I'm ver-y good at in-te-gral and dif-fer-en-tial cal-cu-lus; I
Then I can write a wash-ing bill in Bab-y-lon-ic cu-nei-form, And

know the sci-en-tif-ic names of be-ings an-i-mal-cu-lous: } In
tell you ev-'ry de-tail of Ca-rac-ta-cus-'s u-ni-form:

short, in mat-ters veg-e-ta-ble, an-i-mal, and min-er-al, I

am the ver-y mod-el of a mod-ern Ma-jor-Gen-er-al.

Slower   MG:

3. In fact, when I know what is meant by "mam - e - lon" and "rav - e - lin", When I can tell at sight a Mau - ser ri - fle from a jav - e - lin, When such af - fairs as sor - ties and sur - pris - es I'm more wa - ry at, And when I know pre - cise - ly what is meant by "com-mis - sa - ri - at", When I have learnt what prog-ress has been

pp

58

CHORUS:

an - i - mal, and min - er - al, I am the ver - y mod - el of a mod - ern Ma - jor - Gen - er - al. But

still, in mat - ters veg - e - ta - ble, an - i - mal, and min - er - al, He is the ver - y mod - el of a

mod - ern Ma - jor - Gen - er - al.

If You Give Me Your Attention

PRINCESS IDA

Words by W.S. Gilbert
Music by Arthur Sullivan

1. If you give me your at - ten - tion, I will tell you what I am: I'm a gen - u - ine phi - lan - thro - pist, all
2. To com - pli - ments in - flat - ed I've a with - er - ing re - ply, And van - i - ty I al - ways do my
3. I'm sure I'm no as - cet - ic; I'm as pleas - ant as can be; You'll al - ways find me read - y with a

Copyright © 2001 by HAL LEONARD CORPORATION
International Copyright Secured   All Rights Reserved

62

oth - er kinds are sham. Each lit - tle fault of tem - per and each
best to mor - ti - fy; A char - i - ta - ble ac - tion I can
crush - ing rep - ar - tee. I've an ir - ri - tat - ing chuck - le, I've a

so - ci - al de - fect In my err - ing fel - low crea - tures, I en -
skil - ful - ly dis - sect; And ___ in - ter - est - ed mo - tives I'm de -
cel - e - brat - ed sneer, I've an en - ter - tain - ing snig - ger, I've a

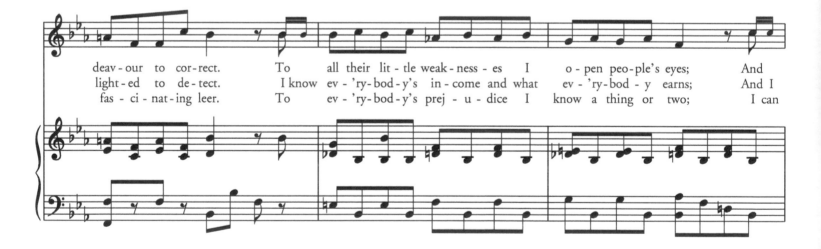

deav - our to cor - rect. To all their lit - tle weak - ness - es I o - pen peo - ple's eyes; And
light - ed to de - tect. I know ev - 'ry - bod - y's in - come and what ev - 'ry - bod - y earns; And I
fas - ci - nat - ing leer. To ev - 'ry - bod - y's prej - u - dice I know a thing or two; I can

lit - tle plans to snub the self - suf - fi - cient I de - vise; I
care - ful - ly com - pare it with the in - come tax re - turns; But to
tell a wom - an's age in half a min - ute, and I do. But al -

love my fel - low crea - tures, I do all the good I can,   Yet
ben - e - fit hu - man - i - ty how - ev - er much I plan,   Yet
though I try to make my - self as pleas - ant as I can,   Yet

1, 2

ev - 'ry - bod - y says I'm such a dis - a - gree - able man! And I can't think why!
ev - 'ry - bod - y says I'm such a dis - a - gree - able man! And I can't think why!
ev - 'ry - bod - y says I am a dis - a - gree - able man! And I

3

can't think why!   I can't think

why!

Whene'er I Spoke
PRINCESS IDA

Words by W.S. Gilbert
Music by Arthur Sullivan

Copyright © 2003 by HAL LEONARD CORPORATION
International Copyright Secured   All Rights Reserved

peo - ple mild Po - lite - ly smil'd, And vo - ted me de - light - ful!

Now when a wight Sits up all night Ill -

na - tur'd jokes de - vis - ing, And all his wiles Are met with smiles, It's

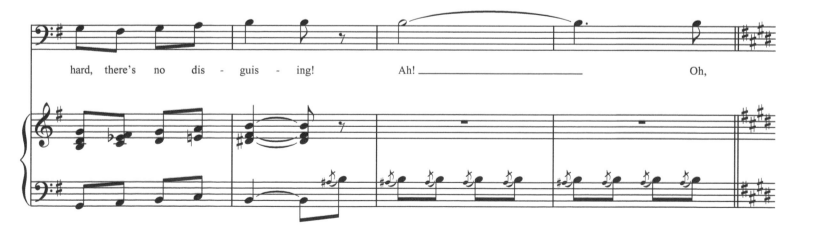

hard, there's no dis - guis - ing! Ah! _____ Oh,

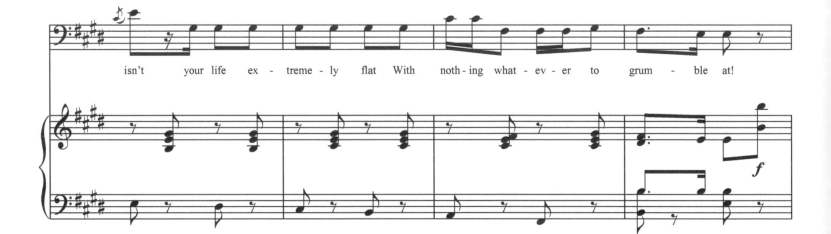

don't the days seem lank and long When all goes right and noth-ing goes wrong, And

isn't your life ex - treme-ly flat With noth-ing what-ev-er to grum - ble at!

2. When Ger - man bands From mu - sic stands Play'd Wag - ner im - per -

fect - ly— I bade them go— They did - n't say no, But off they went di -

rect - ly! The or - gan boys They

stopp'd their noise, With read - i - ness sur - pris - ing, And grin - ning herds of

hur - dy - gurds Re - tired a - po - lo - gis - ing! Ah,————————— Oh,

don't   the days seem lank and long   When all goes right and noth-ing goes wrong,   And

isn't   your life ex-treme-ly flat   With noth-ing what-ev-er to grum-ble at!

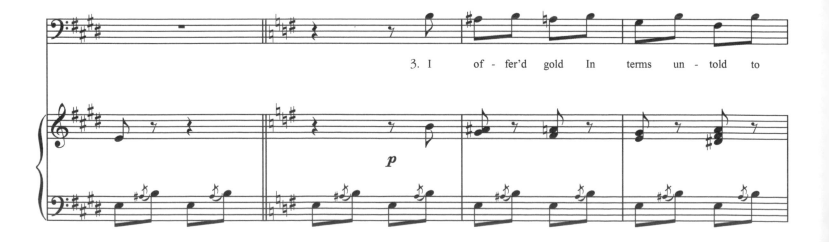

3. I   of-fer'd gold   In terms un-told   to

all who'd con - tra - dict me— I said I'd pay A pound a day To

a - ny - one who kick'd me— I

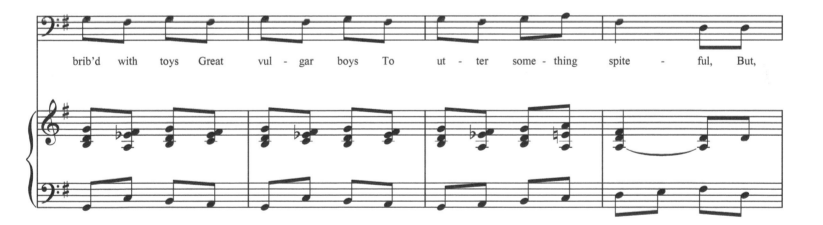

brib'd with toys Great vul - gar boys To ut - ter some - thing spite - ful, But,

bless you, no! They *would* be so Con - foun - ded - ly po - lite - ful!

70

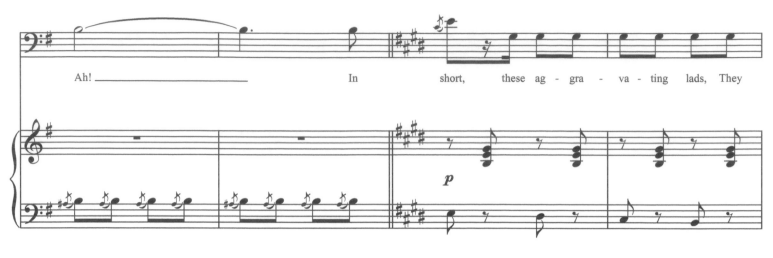

Ah! _____ In short, these ag - gra - va - ting lads, They

tic - kle my tastes, they feed my fads, They give me this and they give me that, And I've

noth - ing what - ev - er to grum - ble at!

My Boy, You May Take It from Me

RUDDIGORE

Words by W.S. Gilbert
Music by Arthur Sullivan

Copyright © 2001 by HAL LEONARD CORPORATION
International Copyright Secured   All Rights Reserved

worst.
gain.
place.

Though clev - er as clev - er can be—
I've a high - ly in - tel - li - gent face—
Then I sing and I play and I paint:

A
My
Though

Crich - ton of ear - ly ro - mance—
fea - tures can - not be de - nied—
none are ac - com-plished as I,

You must stir it and stump it, And
But, what - ev - er I try, sir, I
To say so were trea - son: You

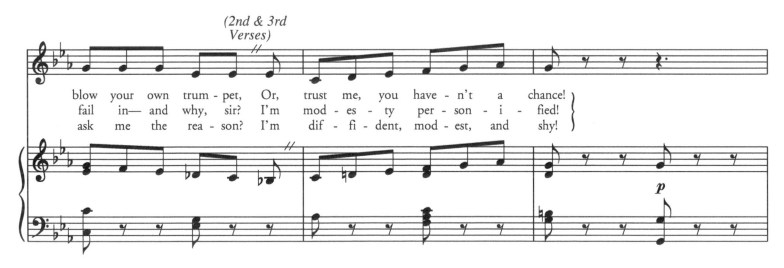

(2nd & 3rd Verses)

blow your own trum - pet, Or, trust me, you have - n't a chance!
fail in— and why, sir? I'm mod - es - ty per - son - i - fied!
ask me the rea - son? I'm dif - fi - dent, mod - est, and shy!

p

If you wish in the world to ad - vance, Your

pp

mer - its you're bound to en - hance, You must stir it and stump it, And

blow your own trum-pet, Or, trust me, you have-n't a chance! chance! If you

wish in the world to ad - vance, Your _____ mer - its you're bound to en - hance, You must

stir it and stump it, And blow your own trum-pet, Or, trust me, you have-n't a chance!

Time Was, When Love and I

THE SORCERER

Words by W.S. Gilbert
Music by Arthur Sullivan

Copyright © 2001 by HAL LEONARD CORPORATION
International Copyright Secured   All Rights Reserved

None bet-ter-loved than I in all the land! Time

was, when maid-ens of the no-blest sta - tion, For - sak-ing e -ven mil - i-tar-y

men, Would gaze up-on me, rapt in a-do-ra - tion— Ah

me, ah me, I was a fair_ young_ cu - rate then!

Had I a head-ache? sighed — the maids as -

sem - bled; Had I a cold? welled forth the si - lent tear;

Did I look pale? then half a par - ish trem - bled; And when I coughed all thought the

opt.

end was near! I had no care— no jeal-ous doubts hung o'er me, For

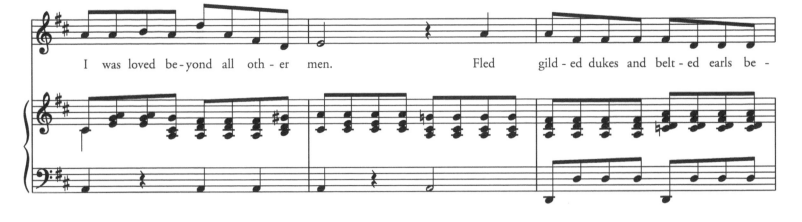

I was loved be-yond all oth-er men. Fled gild-ed dukes and belt-ed earls be -

fore ___ me, Ah me, ah me, I was a pale ___ young ___ cu - rate

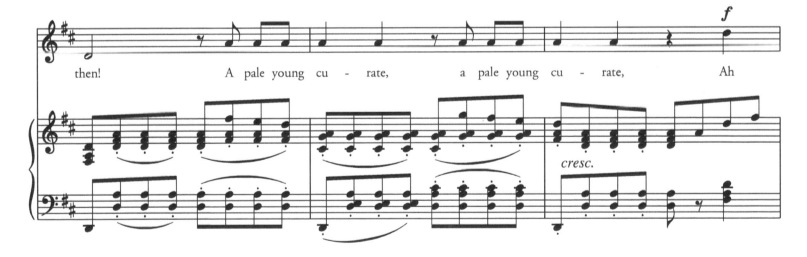

then! A pale young cu - rate, a pale young cu - rate, Ah

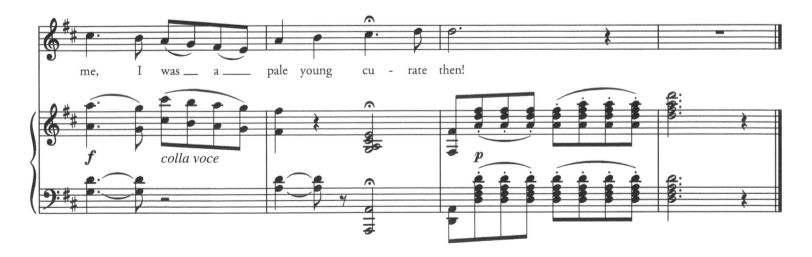

me, I was ___ a ___ pale young cu - rate then!

Engaged to So-and-So

THE SORCERER

Words by W.S. Gilbert
Music by Arthur Sullivan

DR. DALY:

Oh, my voice is sad and

low, And with ti - mid step I go— For with

Copyright © 2003 by HAL LEONARD CORPORATION
International Copyright Secured   All Rights Reserved

load   of love o'er - la - den   I en - quire   of   ev' - ry

maid - en,   "Will you   wed me,   lit - tle   la - dy,   Will you

share   my   cot - tage   sha - dy?"   Lit - tle   la - dy   an - swers

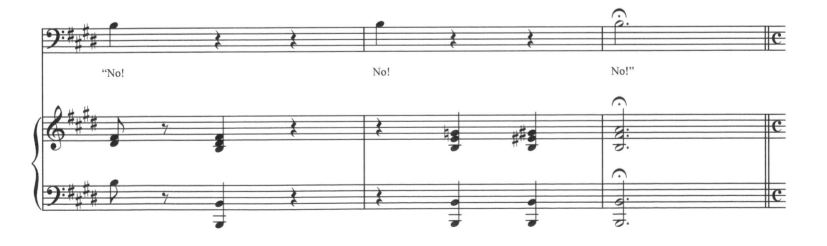

"No!   No!   No!"

Andante moderato

"Thank you for your kind-ly prof-fer— Good your heart, and full your cof-fer;

Yet, I must de-cline your of-fer— I'm en-gag'd to So - and-so!"

So - and-so! So - and-so!

So - and-so! So - and-so!

She's en - gag'd to So - and - so!

What a rogue young hearts to pil - lage! What a work - er on Love's til - lage!

Ev - 'ry maid - en in the vil - lage Is en - gag'd to So - and - so!

82

So - and-so! So - and-so!

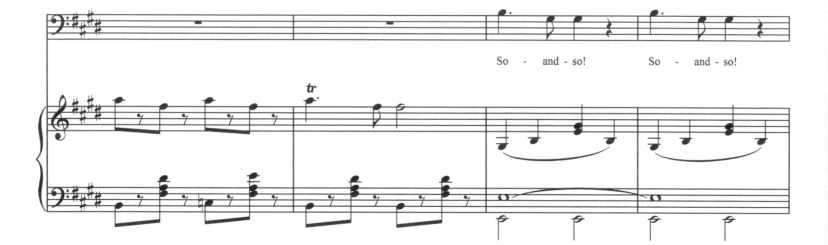

So - and-so! So - and-so!

All en - gag'd to So - and-so!

My Name Is John Wellington Wells

THE SORCERER

Words by W.S. Gilbert
Music by Arthur Sullivan

Copyright © 2001 by HAL LEONARD CORPORATION
International Copyright Secured   All Rights Reserved

bless - ings and curs - es, And ev - er - filled purs - es, In proph - e - cies, witch - es, and knells. _____ If you

want a proud foe to "make tracks"— _____ If you'd melt a rich un - cle in wax— _____ You've

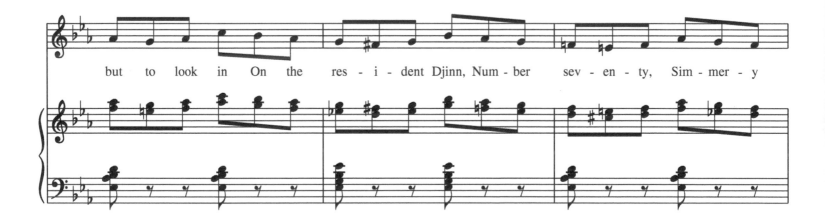

but to look in On the res - i - dent Djinn, Num - ber sev - en - ty, Sim - mer - y

Axe. _____ We've a first - rate as - sort - ment of mag - ic; And for rais - ing a post - hu - mous

shade, With ef - fects that are com - ic or trag - ic, There's no cheap - er house in the

trade. _____ Love - phil - tre, we've quan - ti - ties of it! And for know - ledge if an - y one

burns, _____ We're keep - ing a ver - y small proph - et, a proph - et Who brings us un - bound - ed re -

turns: _____ For he can proph - e - sy With a wink *of* his eye, Peep with se - cu - ri - ty

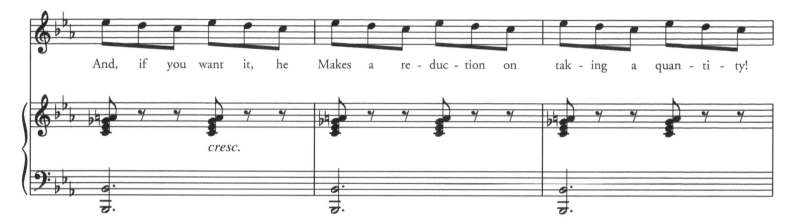

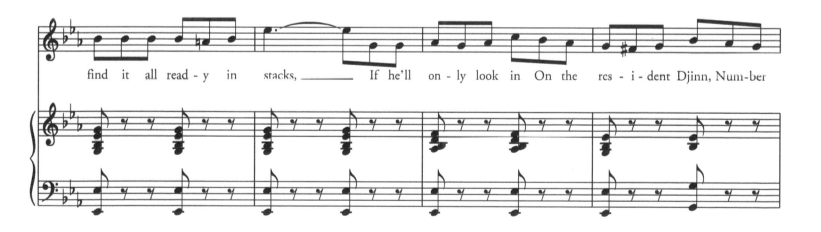

He can raise you hosts Of ghosts, And that, with-out re-flec-tors; And creep-y things With wings, And gaunt and gris-ly spec-tres; He can fill you crowds Of shrouds, And

hor - ri - fy you vast - ly; He can rack your brains With chains, _____ And

gib - ber - ings grim and ghast - ly! Then, if you plan it, he Chang - es or - gan - i - ty,

With an ur - ban - i - ty Full of sa - tan - i - ty, Vex - es hu - man - i - ty

With an in - an - i - ty Fa - tal to van - i - ty, Driv - ing your foes to the

verge of in-san-i-ty! Bar-ring tau-tol-o-gy, In de-mon-ol-o-gy,

'Lec-tro bi-ol-o-gy, Mys-tic no-sol-o-gy; Spir-it phil-ol-o-gy, High-class as-trol-o-gy,

rit.

f *a tempo*

Such is his know-ledge, he Is-n't the man to re - quire an a-pol-o-gy! Oh! _____

cresc. *rit.* **f** *a tempo* *dim.*

_____ My name is John Wel-ling-ton Wells, _____ I'm a deal-er in mag-ic and

p

I've Jibe and Joke
THE YEOMEN OF THE GUARD

Words by W.S. Gilbert
Music by Arthur Sullivan

Copyright © 2001 by HAL LEONARD CORPORATION
International Copyright Secured   All Rights Reserved

I ply my craft And know no fear, But aim my shaft At prince or peer. At

peer or prince— at prince or peer, I aim my shaft and

know no fear!

rall.

Allegretto, non troppo vivace ♩ = 84

1. I've   wis-dom from the East and from the
  set   a   brag-gart quail-ing with a

West,   That's sub-ject to no ac-a-dem-ic rule;   You may
quip,   The up-start I can with-er with a whim;   He may

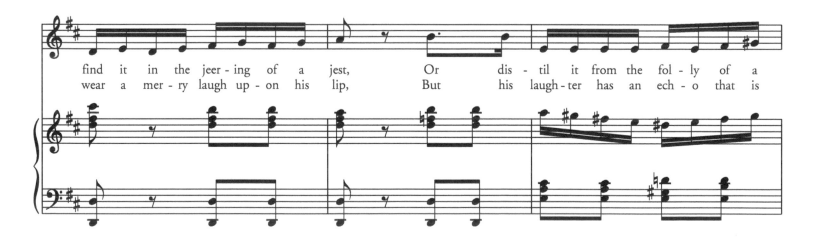

find it in the jeer-ing of a   jest,   Or dis-til it from the fol-ly of a
wear a mer-ry laugh up-on his lip,   But   his laugh-ter has an ech-o that is

fool.   I can teach you with a quip; if I've a mind;   I can
grim!   When they're of-fered to the world in mer-ry guise,   Un -

trick you in - to learn - ing with a laugh; Oh,
pleas - ant truths are swal - lowed with a will, For

win - now all my fol - ly, fol - ly,
he who'd make his fel - low, fel - low,

fol - ly, and you'll find A grain or two of truth a - mong the chaff! Oh,
fel - low crea - tures wise Should al - ways gild the phil - o - soph - ic pill! For

win - now all my fol - ly, fol - ly, fol - ly, and you'll find A grain or two of truth a - mong the
he who'd make his fel - low, fel - low, fel - low crea - tures wise Should al - ways glid the phil - o - soph - ic

chaff!
pill!

2. I can